~

# *The Rats of Hamelin*
## *Forget the Pied-Piper, this is what really happened.*

~

*A play in two acts by*

*H M Sealey*

*From an original idea by*
**Amy Courtenay**

# Cast

## The Rats.

**Fang** – *leader of the rats*
**Sharkey** – *a kinder, more thoughtful rat, although not too bright.*
**Sabretooth** – *a bit of a bully and a show-off. Sharkey's brother.*
**Thorn** – *Fang's second-in-command.*
**Bramble** – *Thorn's sister, a particularly clever rat.*
**Claw** – *A stupid rat, Sabretooth's sidekick.*
**Scratch** – *One of Fang's friends.*
**Killer** – *Another of Sabretooth's cronies. Admires Sabretooth.*

*The rats are quite vicious and greedy. They hate the mice but stay on friendly terms with the cats to save them the bother of being chased.*

## The Mice

**Big Cheese** – *The leader of the mice*
**Squeaker** – *Big Cheese's best friend.*
**Lulu** – *A clever mouse.*
**Sunny** – *A happy, optimistic mouse.*
**Twitch** – *Lulu's brother.*
**Snuffles** – *An old mouse.*
**Maisy** – *One of Lulu's friends.*
**Truffle** – *Another of Lulu's friends.*

*The mice are quite harmless and kind creatures. They try to stay hidden from both the rats and the cats.*

## The Cats

**Tom** – *The leader of the cats. Clever but lazy.*
**Captain** – *Old fashioned, kind and military minded.*
**Tabby** – *One of Tom's friends.*
**Fluff** – *Tabby's best friend.*
**Kitty** – *A little quieter than the others.*
**Whiskers** – *A lazy, greedy cat.*

*The cats are reasonably lazy and selfish. They prefer not to have to chase the rats, but they are all very fond of eating mice*

## Other Characters

*The voices of people are often heard though not seen. The Pied Piper's voice is also heard.*

*There can be as many or as few rats, cats and mice as desired.*

## THE RATS of HAMLIN

### Act One

**Scene one**

*A sign reads* **"Hamelin's Premier Cheese shop."**
*There are all sorts of cheeses lying around.*
*Several large rats are supposed to be standing guard, carrying weapons, but they are all asleep, slumped on top of the cheeses, snoring loudly. Two of the rats are* **Sabretooth** *and* **Killer.**

**Big Cheese, Squeaker** *and* **lulu** *enter on tiptoe.* **Squeaker** *flashes a torch around. They are accompanied by other mice. They spot the cheese.*

**Big Cheese :** *(whispering)* Shhhh! Everyone be quiet.

**Lulu :** What if they wake up? They'll bite our tails off if they catch us. I like my tail.

3

**Squeaker :** There's no point in having cheese if we ain't got our tails boss.

**Big Cheese :** Jeez! Are you two mice or men? Besides these rotten rats don't have any right to keep all the cheese to themselves. Now, move quickly. Take as much as you can. We've got a lot of hungry mouths to feed.

**Lulu :** Rats are horrible! They're big and ugly.

**Squeaker :** And they keep eating all the cheese!

**Lulu :** That's because they're greedy

**Squeaker :** And stinky.

**Lulu and Squeaker :**
*(giggling)* Can anyone tell me the point of a rat?
They don't have the whiskers or speed of a cat.
They haven't got wings and they haven't got stings
They sound pretty lousy when one of them sings.
They're lacking in cuteness, in smarts and in style,
And try not to mention that snaggle-toothed smile.
They're clumsy and graceless.
And tacky and tasteless.
There's no other word to describe them but vile!

**Big Cheese :** Shut up you two and get moving!

*The mice begin to roll the cheese offstage. The rats give the occasional snuffle and yawn and the mice freeze, then continue to take the cheese.*
*Once the room is almost empty,* **Lulu** *and* **Squeaker** *tiptoe over to the sleeping rats and tie their tails together.*

**Big Cheese :** That's it. We're done. C'mon guys.

*As the mice sneak out,* **Squeaker** *falls over a left over piece of cheese and crashes into a shelf or other noisy piece of scenery. The*

4

*Rats wake up suddenly.*

**Sabretooth :** Hey! *(suddenly realising the mice have taken the cheese)* Hey! Give us back our cheese you little pipsqueaks!

**Big Cheese** *runs offstage.* **Lulu** *and* **Squeaker** *pause and stick out their tongues. The rats leap up without realising their tails are tied together. They fall in a heap on the floor. The mice escape.*

**Squeaker :** See you around, you big ugly morons.

*The rats shake their fists and shout after the mice.*

**Killer :** Oh great. We lost the cheese.

**Sabretooth :** What'd'you mean *we*? *You* lost the cheese, you big dumb rodent. You were asleep.

**Killer :** I was not asleep. I was......waiting to pounce. I just waited a bit too long.

**Sabretooth :** Do you always snore when you're waiting to pounce?

**Killer :** Well, why didn't you stop them then?

**Sabretooth :** I didn't hear them sneak in. You were snoring too loudly. An elephant could have come thundering in and I would still only have heard you grunting like a pig in the corner.

**Killer :** Fang's gonna be real angry with us. He'll throw us to the cats and there'll be nothing left of us but whiskers.

**Sabretooth :** Mice! Thieving vermin. Stealing our cheese like that.

**Killer :** Yeah. *(pause)* Sabretooth? Didn't *we* steal the cheese in the first place?

**Sabretooth :** No. *(pause)* Maybe. A bit. Come on, lets go tell Fang the bad news.

5

*(They stand up forgetting their tails are still tied together, then fall over again.)*
And let's not tell him about our tails. Makes you look kinda dumb.

**Killer :** Me? What about you?

**Sabretooth :** Well, *you're* tied to *me* aren't you?

*Killer thinks about this.*

**Killer :** I guess I am.

**Sabretooth.** *(Pulling Killer offstage by the tail)* Quite. It would've been a different story if they'd tried to tie me to you. They probably wouldn't have dared. Even a stupid mouse can see I'm not to be tangled with. See these teeth? Teeth of death, they call them.

**Killer :** Who calls them?

**Sabretooth :** Everyone!

*exit both,* **Sabretooth** *is still boasting.*

**End of scene one**


**Scene two.**

**Big Cheese's** *Squeakeasy.*

*The mice sit on seats made of upturned cotton-reels etc. The girls dance in a chorus line. The Mouse band play instruments made from everyday objects. In the corner there are two signs, red circles with a line across, one of a rat, one of a cat.*
**Lulu, Truffle, Maisy, Sunny** *and the girls sing. Cheese is offered on plates.*

**Girls :**

6

There's a word that we've heard,
There's a word that we adore.
It's the only word we ever need.
No word could matter more.
The word is "Squeak."
It's the word we speak!
Every day of every week.
As vocab goes it's quite unique.
Squeak's a term you have to learn.
We say it all the time.
Squeak means "go" and Squeak means "no,"
And Squeak means "yes I'm fine."
The word is "Squeak."
It's the word we speak,
Every day of every week.
Without it no mouse is complete.

**Big Cheese, Snuffles** *and* **Twitch** *sit together looking pleased with themselves.* **Snuffles** *nibbles on the cheese.*

**Snuffles :** Hmmm. Mature cheddar. A very fine nose indeed.

**Big Cheese :** We got a good lot last night. Spread the word. Big Cheese's Squeakeasy is the *only* place to come for a nibble of cheese.

**Twitch :** weren't you scared of the rats boss?

**Big Cheese :** Pshaw! Rats shmats. I'm not scared of those overgrown gerbils. I'm Big Cheese. I've been in charge of Hamelin's cheese supply for ten years. Yes sirree, those Rats had better stay off my turf.

**Twitch :** I dunno boss. I hear Fang wants to chase all the mice out of Hamlin. He wants all the cheese for himself.

**Big Cheese :** Fang? That crooked-toothed furball doesn't scare me. Why, I'm more scared of an itty-bitty ladybird than I am of him. *(shouting)* The cheese is on the house everyone!

*Everyone cheers. Suddenly,* **Squeaker** *rushes in, looking frightened. He looks around until he sees* **Big Cheese***, and hurries to him.*

**Squeaker :** *(trying not to speak too loudly)* The rats are coming!

**Big Cheese :** *(struggling to hear over the noise)* What?

**Squeaker :** *(a little louder)* I said the rats are coming!

**Big Cheese :** I can't hear you. Speak louder.

**Twitch :** I think he said something about hats, boss.

**Big Cheese :** *(pushing his hat back proudly)* Well thanks. I like my hat too.

**Squeaker :** I said rats. The Rats are coming.

**Snuffles :** You're mumbling. All young people mumble today.

**Squeaker :** *(getting impatient)* I said THE RATS ARE COMING!

*As* **Squeaker** *shouts the warning, the Squeakeasy falls silent for a moment. Then everyone looks horrified. All the mice look at one another and the word "rats" is echoed around the room.*

**Big Cheese :** Rats! Coming here? Why didn't you say so? *(Addressing all the mice)* Now, no-one panic.

**Twitch :** Rats? The boss ain't scared of no rats. Right boss?

**Twitch** *turns to* **Big Cheese,** *but* **Big Cheese** *has already run away. Suddenly the rats flood the stage. The chase the mice, kick over the stools and steal the cheese. The Mice scream and run away, chased by the Rats.*

*Three of the mice find themselves trapped by* **Sabretooth, Killer, Claw** *and* **Sharkey** *who chase them around. The other rats lounge* *around eating the cheese and laughing.*

**Killer :** I'll teach you mice to tie *my* tail.

**Sabretooth :** I don't think they need your help with that.

*The other rats laugh*

**Killer :** They made me look like a right idiot.

**Sabretooth :** I don't think *you* need any help with that.

*The rats roar with laughter*

**Killer :** There's still a knot in my poor tail.

*The rats chase the mice once again*

**Sabretooth  :** *(laughing)* Look at the three dumb mice!

**Claw :** *(echoing him)* Three dumb mice!

**Sabretooth :** See how they run!

**Claw :** See how they run!

**Claw** *and* **Sabretooth** *suddenly realise that they are almost quoting a poem and they laugh*

**Killer :** I ought to chop off their tails!

**Sabretooth :**  With a carving knife!

**Claw :** With a carving knife!

**Sabretooth  :** *(enjoying the joke)* Did you ever see such a thing in your life?

*The three mice finally manage to escape,* **Killer** *exits too, following* *them.* **Sharkey** *watches them go but doesn't look as happy as the other rats.*

**Sharkey :** *(not understanding the reference)* What?

**Sabretooth :** What?

**Claw :** What?

**Shark :** What thing did you see?

**Sabretooth :** What?

**Sharkey :** What did you mean? Did you ever see such a thing in your life?

**Claw, Sabretooth** *and the other Rats groan*

**Sabretooth :** I swear you're dumber than Killer and Claw put together. Have you got a brain in your head Sharkey? Or is it all just teeth?

**Claw :** All teeth?

*(The Rats laugh)*

**Sabretooth :** It was a *nursery rhyme*, you overgrown mouse. You know, a song.

**Sharkey.** *(thinks about this.)* Oh. *(pause)* But you weren't singing.

**Sabretooth :** Jeez! *Everyone* knows Three Blind Mice.

**Claw :** Everyone.

**Sharkey :** *(looks around)* Where?

**Claw :** Where's what?

10

**Sharkey :** The three blind mice? Were they blind?

**Sabretooth :** It's not so much Three Blind Mice with you as One Stupid Rat.

**Claw :** Stupid rat.

*Everyone laughs at* **Sharkey,** *then, suddenly, they fall silent when* **Fang, Thorn, Bramble** *and* **Scratch** *enter.*

**Fang :** So this is where the little thieves have been hiding out.

*The rats bring* **Fang** *a seat.*

**Thorn :** I don't like it. It's too – mousy.

**Bramble :** And it's dark and poky.

**Scratch :** Of course its dark and poky, it's a mousehole.

**Fang :** We can soon fix that. It's ours now.
*the rats put up a big sign that reads – Under new management. No mice!*

**Thorn :** I mean, look at this joint. Eww! Don't mice have any sense of style?

**Sabretooth :** Mice don't have any sense at all.
*The Rats all laugh except* **Fang** *who likes to be the one too make the jokes*

**Thorn :** I declare this property of Fang.

*The Rats cheer*

**Scratch :** It won't be long before we drive every mouse out of Hamlin chief.

*The rats cheer again*

**Thorn :** *(With hero-worship)* And then Fang will be King of the whole town.

*The rats cheer again*

**Fang :** I hate mice. They give vermin a bad name. All squeaky and cute. I mean what's with the squeaking anyway? *(speaking in a high-pitched voice)* ooh, look at me everyone, I'm so fluffy and my whiskers are twitchy. Oooh, I should be in a Disney cartoon wearing a stupid hat.

*All the rats find this very funny indeed.*

**Sharkey :** I wonder where they're all going?

**Scratch :** Who cares, as long as they get their cute little backsides out of Hamelin. We don't want their sort here.

**Bramble :** You can say that again.

**Scratch :** We don't want their sort here.

**Sharkey :** Why don't we?

**Fang :** What did you just say?

**Sabretooth :** That's just my brother Sharkey boss. He's as dumb as a mouse himself.    The runt of the litter.

**Claw :** Runt of the litter.

**Sharkey :** I just wondered why we're suddenly trying to chase all the mice out of Hamelin. Mice and rats have always lived together.

**Thorn :** But why should we live together?

**Bramble :** Mice are an evolutionary dead-end.

*The rats look a little confused.*

**Sabretooth :** They're a what now?

**Bramble :** Well, they're....*(stops, realising that the rats are not understanding)*Oh never mind. They're smaller than us.

**Scratch :** And they're weaker than us. We rats are far stronger. We should have the best food and the most comfortable homes.

*The rats all cheer and shout their agreement*

**Thorn :** Fang thinks its time we stopped being scavengers and started taking charge of this dump of a town. The mice need to get out of our way.

**Scratch :** There ain't enough cheese in this town for all of us.

**Sharkey :** *(quietly)* We could all share the cheese.

**Fang :** I'm the boss of the rats, and I say I've had enough *sharing* with those twitchy- nosed little squirts. It's time we rats overran this whole town. I want all the townspeople to run away screaming when they see us!

**Thorn :** We'll bite the goats!

**Sabretooth :** And eat the oats!

**Bramble :** And scare the fishermen in the boats.

**Scratch :** We'll gnaw the fruit!

**Sabretooth :** We'll sup the soup!

**Bramble :** And kill the chickens in the coop!

**Thorn :** We'll chew the meat!

13

**Sabretooth :** And chase the sheep!

**Scratch :** And gnaw the barley and the wheat.

**Thorn :** We'll say it once.

**Bramble :** We'll say it twice.

**Rats :** We'll rid the town of all the mice!

**Killer** *enters, his head stuck in what looks like a piece of pipe. He staggers around unable to see until* **Sabretooth** *and* **Claw** *pull the pipe off his head.*

**Killer :** I nearly got 'em. Only they went up the drainpipe.

**Sabretooth :** You're too fat to get up a drainpipe. You eat too much cheese.

**Claw :** Too much cheese.

**Fang :** Oh yeah. Talking of cheese. Someone let those miserable excuses for rodents steal all my cheese last night.

*Everyone turns and stares at* **Killer. Killer** *points to* **Sabretooth** *rather pathetically.*

**Killer :** Wasn't me Chief. At least, it wasn't my fault. There were hundreds of 'em. Great big mice they were. In fact, they might not have been mice at all, thinking about it. They might have been dogs.

**Fang :** That was *my* cheese.

**Killer :** I'll get you some more cheese Chief.

**Fang :** You're a laughing stock, Killer. And you work for me so that makes me a laughing stock.

**Killer :** You ain't a laughing stock Chief.

**Fang :** I ain't a laughing stock because I don't let idiots like you work for me.

**Killer :** Don't throw me to the cats Chief. I swear I'll get you your cheese.

**Fang :** Too late.

**Fang** *snaps his fingers or makes some other signal and* **Thorn** *and* **Scratch** *grab* **Killer** *and drag him out.*

**Killer :** No! Please Chief. Anything but the cats!

**Sharkey** *looks upset by this but* **Sabretooth** *makes a gesture that tells him to keep quiet*

**Sabretooth :** They'll throw you to the cats too little brother, if you don't start acting more like a rat.

**Sharkey :** I just don't see why we can't share the cheese. That's all.

**Bramble :** Because that's the way nature works dummy! The strongest get the cheese, the weakest die out. Evolution. Survival of the fittest.

**Sabretooth :** *(obviously not understanding a word)* Yeah. Just what I was about to say.

**Fang :** All right you miserable bunch of hamsters! Get out there and terrorise the town. Scare the girls and chase the boys.
Chew the heads off all their toys.
Fill the town with frightened noise!
Snarl and spit and snap and squeak.
Bite and gnaw and shout and shriek.
Find some naughtiness to wreak.

**All Rats :** Yes Chief!

*The rats all scurry away.* **Fang** *picks up a piece of cheese, bites into it, and exits*

**End of scene two**


**Scene three.**

*The stage is in darkness. A woman screams.*

**Voice :** A rat! It's a rat! Someone kill it!

*More voices join in, along with the squeaking of rats and the pattering of paws. The rats can scamper through the audience and generally cause chaos.*

**Voice :** There are rats in my house, someone chase them away!

**Voice :** That's no fluffy mouse! Its enormous and grey!

**Voice :** They're scaring the children and eating the cheese!

**Voice :** Somebody do something! Kill them all, please!

**Voice :** They're vermin! They'll bring in the plague I declare!

**Voice :** They're gnawing my toes! Fetch the Mayor! Fetch the Mayor!

**Voice :** They're all over Hamlin! They've shredded my blouses!

**Voice :** They're making their beds from our knickers and trousers!

**Voice :** Somebody stop them! They need to be shot!

**All voices together :** Won't somebody help us and slaughter the lot?!

**End of scene three.**

**Scene four.**

*The Cats' favourite spot.* **Tom, Tabby, Fluff, Whiskers** *and* **Kitty** *sit calmly and lazily on top of dustbins. From here they can watch the world pass by.*

**Tabby :** *(discarding what looks like a rat's tail)* That last rat was far too stringy.

**Tom :** I agree. The quality of the rats has gone shamefully downhill lately.

**Fluff :** What I fancy is a small, tender, succulent mouse. So much more flavour than rat.

**Tom :** Ah. Mouse. Delicious. The problem is, mice are very clever and small enough to hide in the tiniest of places. The rats on the other hand are bigger and quite stupid.

**Tabby :** And stringy.

**Tom :** Far too stringy.

**Kitty :** Has anyone else noticed something strange recently?

**Whiskers :** I noticed my fur looks particularly glossy recently.

**Fluff :** Strange?

**Kitty :** The people aren't their usual slow-witted selves. They all
17

seem upset about something.

**Tabby :** *(laughing)* They're people! What have they got to be upset about?

**Fluff :** They eat. They sleep. They give us milk and stroke our fur. They aren't clever enough to do anything else.

**Tabby :** Exactly. We take care of the poor, stupid, two-legged creatures.

**Fluff :** They haven't even got whiskers! Can you imagine not having whiskers?

**Whiskers :** They're terribly dull and ugly. That's why they need us.

**Kitty :** Well, I think the people seem very upset.

**Tom :** If there's trouble in Hamelin I should be the first to know. Where's Captain? He ought to be back by now.

**Fluff :** You know Captain, he's probably stopped off for a sly saucer of milk somewhere.

**Tabby :** Or for a quick ball of string.

**Captain** *enters and crashes into the dustbins. He's a distinguished old army cat.*

**Captain :** Sir! Sir! We've got problems sir! Big problems!

**Kitty :** I told you so.

**Tom :** What sort of problems?

**Captain :** It's the rats sir.

**Tom :** The rats? What about them?

**Captain :** They're taking over sir! 'Undreds of the blighters sir. Big, 'orrible rats. Coming out of everywhere they are. Like a swarm sir, a bally swarm.

**Tom :** Taking over?

**Captain :** You should see 'em sir. You should hear 'em. All the squeaking and shrieking. And all the people running in all directions. Been kicked twice by their great big feet I have sir. And my poor tail's been trodden on more often than a carpet sir. It's chaos I tell you.

**Tom :** It seems our rodent friends are getting bold.

**Fluff :** I thought we had a deal with the rats?

**Tabby :** Yeah, me too.

**Tom :** We do indeed have a deal with the rats. They keep away from bothering our people too much, and in return, we don't bother them too much.

**Fluff :** That's right. Otherwise our people would start telling us to catch the rats.

**Tabby :** And catching rats is a waste of our valuable time.

**Fluff :** And tiring.

**Whiskers :** And undignified. Sewers and drains, that's where the rats live. Do I look like the sort of cat who frequents sewers and drains?

**Kitty :** No, you look like the sort of cat who frequents larders and storecupboards.

**Whiskers :** Are you suggesting I'm fat?

**Kitty :** Well, I'm not the one who got her bottom stuck in the cat flap last week.

**Whiskers :** It was a very small cat flap!

**Captain :** Anyway, them rodents aren't honouring no deal sir. That they're not. Racing around Hamlin like furry grey bullets they are sir. Into everything. Eating the cheese, chasing the dogs. Not that I like dogs myself sir, but you have to feel for the poor beasts being set upon by a swarm of rats sir. Its those big yellow teeth sir. 'Orrible they are.

**Tom :** Thieving, lying, worthless creatures!

**Fluff :** Ugly, cheating, buck-toothed leeches!

**Tabby :** Never trust a rat, they'll lie to you like that.

**Fluff :** If you want someone to trust then choose a cat.

**Captain :** Underhanded little blighters!

**Tabby :** Vicious, snarling, big-eared fighters.

**Fluff :** Moth-eaten and scabby, and mangy and shabby.

**Tabby :** Not like a smart, clever tabby.

**Kitty :** But why? The rats don't want us to go back to chasing them any more than we do.

**Captain :** I'm not sure I know ma'am. All I know is they're running riot.

**Tom :** It looks to me as if the rats have forgotten their place. I think we need to remind them who's really in charge of Hamelin.

**Cats :** Yes sir!

**End of scene four**

**Scene five.**

*Darkness. The scratching of claws of squealing of the rats is heard. Voices speak in the dark.*

**Voice :** These rats are just dreadful! They're swarming like bugs!

**Voice :** They've stolen the cheese and they've chewed up the rugs.

**Voice :** Where are the cats? Where are Tabby and Tom?

**Voice :** They're lazing inside with a hot fire on.

**Voice :** Wake them up! Lazy things, get them chasing the rats!

**All voices :** If not for rat-catching what use are the cats?

*The sound of cats joins the melee. The rats scatter, shrieking.* **Tom** *and the cats seem rather annoyed.*

**Tom :** Well now, this will never do. I was very comfortable by the fire.

**Fluff :** It's raining outside. I hate chasing rats. They taste terrible.

**Kitty :** Well, we are cats. I think that means we're meant to get rid of the rats.

**Tabby :** This is going to be a dreadful nuisance. My people have threatened to stop giving me milk if I don't get chase the rats away.

**Fluff :** So have mine.

**Whiskers :** I haven't chased a rat since I was a kitten.

**Tom :** Those rodents will pay for this!

*one of the rats,* **Scratch,** *runs past the cats*

**Tabby :** There's one!

**Fluff :** Get him!

**Captain :** Oi you 'orrible little maggot!

*The cats chase* **Scratch** *offstage.*

**End of scene five.**


**Scene six.**

*The Rats' lair. Food and supplies are piled up all around. All the rats except* **Scratch** *and* **Killer** *are in the room, laughing, joking and sharing hunks of cheese.*

**Thorn :** Did you see their faces? *(pretending)* Arghhh! A rat! A horrible rat!

**Sharkey :** Have a piece of cheese. Have another one. There's lots.

**Sabretooth :** We must have almost all the cheese in Hamelin.

**Fang :** So who's the king of Hamelin?

**Claw :** King of Hamelin!

**Rats :** You are Chief!

**Fang :** Look out everyone, here I come.
Who ever said that rats were dumb?
I've got the whole town in my paws.

So wave your tails and raise your claws!

**Thorn :** Who's the boss of Hamelin town?

**Sabretooth :** Who's the guy who wears the crown?

**Sharkey :** Who's the fellow with all the cheese?

**Fang :** That's me! I'm the king of all he sees!

**Bramble :** Who's the chap with all the clout?

**Sabretooth :** Who's this king we've heard about?

**Sharkey :** Who's the guy we all esteem?

**Fang :** That's me! I'm the rat who got the cream!
Look out everyone, hear the buzz,
Hamlin town belongs to us!
I'm the fellow who makes the laws.
Hamelin town is in my paws!

*Everyone cheers and returns to celebrating. Suddenly,* **Scratch**
*rushes in, panting. He is holding his tail over his arm but his tail is
no longer attached to his body.*

**Scratch :** My tail! My beautiful tail! Look at it! Look at what those
mangy, flea-bitten moggies did to my tail.

**Sharkey :** What happened?

**Scratch :** They bit it off! With their great big teeth! They cased me
clean across town. Ooooh my poor, poor tail. Someone put it back.

**Thorn** *takes* **Scratch's** *tail and tries to re-attach it.*

**Sabretooth :** I thought we had an agreement with the cats?

**Claw :** An agreement.

23

**Fang :** Yeah. We keep out of their way and they keep out of ours. That's how we like it.

**Scratch :** Well, they ain't keeping out of our way any more Chief. They sent you a letter. *(produces a letter)*

**Thorn** *takes the letter for* **Fang** *and reads it out.*

**Thorn :** For the attention of the rats -
"It seems you creatures don't recall,
That useful pact between us all.
So just to jog your furry brains,
We'll spell it out for you again.
We cats do not enjoy the chore,
Of chasing rodents – it's a bore.
And rats, we're sure don't find it fun,
To see a cat and have to run.
We'll say we haven't heard a squeak,
If you keep silent and discreet.
But if you scamper through the town,
We cats will have to hunt you down.
So our advice – and don't forget it,
Is STOP or else you will regret it.
Slink back into your homes and then you,
Might not be on our next menu."

**Sabretooth :** They don't seem very pleased Chief.

**Fang :** You just leave the cats to me.

**Sharkey :** I wouldn't be very happy either, if I were a cat. We're not supposed to bother the people of Hamelin then they don't bother us.

**Scratch :** They bothered my tail. They bit it off! It hurts.

**Bramble :** Maybe you'll get used to not having a tail. *(thoughtful)* I wonder if it'll change your aerodynamic properties?

**Sabretooth :** *(not understanding)* It'll make him shorter anyway.

**Thorn :** Never mind your tail. We don't want cats chasing us. They've got enormous great paws.

**Sabretooth :** Enormous great *sharp* paws!

**Fang :** When I took over as chief of the rats, I promised you the cats would never threaten us again. I know how to handle cats. You just trust Fang. After all, I'm the king of Hamlin.

**Scratch :** Not if the cats rip your tail off you won't be.

**Fang :** You just wait and see, all of you. I'll have the cats eating out of my paw before tonight.

**Sabretooth :** You sure Chief?

**Fang :** Are you calling me a liar?

**Sabretooth :** No. No, course I'm not. It's just, well, cats are pretty big Chief. And look what they did to Scratch. We need to keep them on our side.

**Claw :** On our side.

**Fang :** Cats are nothing but great big hairballs with tails. You need brains to deal with a cat, and who has all the brains around here?

**Sabretooth :** Bramble does. *(suddenly realising that was the wrong answer)* I mean you, chief.

**Fang :** Exactly!
Who's the guy with all the schemes?
Who's the brain behind the scenes?

**Sabretooth :** You are Chief.

**Fang :** Who's the guy with the razor-sharp wits?

25

Who's the guy with all the tricks?

**Thorn :** You are Chief.

**Fang :** Who's the scourge of Hamelin's streets?
Who's the guy that no-one beats?

**Scratch :** You are Chief.

**Fang :** Who's the smartest rat of all?
Who's the one the cats daren't maul?

**Rats :** You are Chief.

**Fang :** So listen up and quit your bellyaching gang. I'm going to make those cats an offer they can't refuse. Just wait and see.

*Exit* **Fang** *and the Rats.* **Sharkey** *stays for a few moments and watches them go, looking worried.*

**End of scene six.**

**Scene seven**

*An empty storehouse. Boxes and baskets lie strewn around but there is no food.*
**Squeaker** *and* **Lulu** *enter, looking frightened. They scuttle around the stage for a while, then, once they're sure they're not being followed, they knock on an upturned basket.*
*The basket is thrown back to reveal* **Big Cheese**.

26

**Squeaker :** All clear Boss.

**Big Cheese :** You're sure?

**Lulu :** Absolutely.

**Big Cheese :** Not that I'm scared of the rats. No sir. I'm just concerned for you lot.

**Squeaker :** Of course you are Boss.

**Big Cheese** *hammers on the side of boxes and baskets, and* **Snuffles***,* **Maisy, Twitch, Truffle, Sunny** *and all the other mice emerge*

**Big Cheese :** Okay you guys! Rise and shine. Out you come.

**Sunny :** Is it safe?

**Snuffles :** I never thought I'd have to hide in a barrel that smells of fish. Ugh.

**Truffle :** You're lucky. I don't know what was in my basket I think it had been dead for a very long time.

**Maisy :** Have the rats gone?

**Lulu :** They've gone.

**Twitch :** *(looking around)* They're not the only thing that's gone. There's not a smidgen of food left. Not a crumb of cheese.

**Sunny :** At least they didn't find us.

**Twitch :** We can't go on like this Boss. Pretty soon there'll be no food left in Hamelin.

**Truffle :** I'm hungry.

**Maisy :** Me too.

*The mice crowd around* **Big Cheese**, *complaining*

**Big Cheese :** Okay, okay. Pipe down and let me think.

**Snuffles :** Well, we're starving. You're the boss, you do something.

**Lulu :** They've snaffled the cheeses, they've raided the freezers.

**Truffle :** Those horrible, yellow-toothed louts!

**Squeaker :** They've gobbled the grapes and they've stolen the cakes.

**Maisy :** The only things here are the sprouts.

**Twitch :** We have to have dinner, we're all getting thinner.

**Lulu :** We'll starve if we don't get food soon.

**Squeaker :** That barrel right there has been licked 'til it's bare.

**Truffle :** And all we've got left is the spoon.

**All mice :** *(to Big Cheese)* Make some decisions and get some provisions.
If you don't then you can't be our boss.
You're the big cheese so we're begging you please,
Sort this out or we're gonna get cross!

**Maisy :** I'm so hungry I could eat a rat.

**Lulu :** Urgh! I'd rather starve.

**Truffle :** Well that's okay because it looks like we are going to starve.

**Maisy :** Oh don't say that. I'm scared! *(starts to cry)*

**Sunny :** Don't cry Maisy. Things are never as bad as they seem.

**Lulu :** That's right. The Boss'll do something, won't you boss?

**Big Cheese :** Um, sure. I've got *loads* of ideas.

**Squeaker :** Yeah? Name two.

**Big Cheese :** Well, there's…um, there's….they're a bit complicated to explain, but they're good ideas. Ideas that end up with lots of cheese.

**Sunny :** See? We should try to look on the bright side.

**Twitch :** What bright side? The side where we starve or the side where the rats tear us limb from limb?

**Sunny :** There's always a bright side. Sometimes you just have to smile. Things never seem as bad when you smile.

**End of scene seven**

**Scene eight**

**Tom** *and the cats lounge on their dustbins, waiting.*
**Captain** *enters.*

**Captain :** They're here sir. A whole swarm of 'em. Nasty looking blighters and no mistake. Are you sure you don't just want us to chase them away?

**Tom :** No, no. I want to talk to those impudent furballs. They're either suddenly very brave or very stupid. I want to know which it is.

**Captain :** Stupid sir. I'd stake my whiskers on it. Ah well, whatever you say sir. Let 'em in.

**Fang** *and the rats enter looking very confident. The cats hiss at them.*

**Sabretooth :** Jeez! I forgot how big cats are. They look like elephants with fur.

**Sharkey :** Look at those teeth.

**Thorn :** And those claws!

**Scratch :** Sure is a lot of pointy bits.

**Fang :** Shut up you miserable bunch. I've seen pointier carrots! Anyone would think you were scared of a few stupid cats.

**Tom :** Stupid cats are we?

**Fang :** Stupid? Did anyone say stupid? *(The rats all look innocent and shake their heads)* I didn't say stupid. I said *(thinking quickly)* Stupendous. That's it. Stupendous cats.

*The cats seem unconvinced and begin to gather around the rats*

**Thorn :** Amazing cats!

**Sabretooth :** Awesome cats!

**Scratch :** Splendid and tremendous cats!

**Bramble :** Handsome cats!

**Thorn :** Noble cats!

**Sabretooth :** Delightful and insightful cats!

**Fang :** As you can see, my gang and I have nothing but respect for you cats.

**Tom :** Really? Then why don't you explain why you and your rodent friends have been tearing around Hamlin?

**Tabby :** Frightening the children.

**Fluff :** Biting the dogs.

**Kitty :** Gnawing all the furniture.

**Whiskers :** Scaring the chickens.

**Captain :** Chewing the bedclothes.

**All cats :** Eating all the food!

**Fang :** We're fed up of hiding away in the sewers and drains. We want a little fun.

**Tom :** That's all very well, but the people of Hamlin are blaming us!

**Tabby :** They have this silly idea that cats should keep a town free of rats.

**Fluff :** And now everyone thinks we cats are useless.

**Whiskers :** And lazy.

**Kitty :** Which, to be fair, some of us are.

**Whiskers :** That's not the point. *(to the rats)* It's all your fault.

**Tom :** So give me one good reason why we shouldn't gobble you all up right now, tails and all?

*The cats crowd around the rats*

**Fang :** You *could* gobble us all up. *(clever pause)* But wouldn't you rather have lots of fresh, juicy mice?

**Tom :** Mice?

31

**Captain :** Mice?

**Fluff :** Fresh mice?

**Tabby :** Juicy mice?

**Fang :** As many as you can eat.

**Tom :** When I'm scheming and dreaming I'm thinking of mice. Stir-fried and tender and served up with rice.

**Kitty :** Their ears are like nectar, their tails are divine.

**Fluff :** Some spices and salt and they taste extra-fine.

**Captain :** They taste jolly grand when they're fried in a pan.

**Tom :** And when grilled they're as sweet as can be.

**Tabby :** Curried or fried with some chips on the side.

**Fluff :** Or baked in a pie for our tea.

**All cats :** Give us mice or a mouse, not a pheasant or grouse,
Make it roasted or toasted or stewed.
Our ravenous tums just don't care how it comes,
Just give us our favourite food!

**Tom :** We love mice. But we'll eat rat if we have to.

**Fang :** But you don't have to. I have a little proposition for you cats.

**Tom :** We're listening.

**Fang :** We rats have spent far too long putting up with those useless little creatures running around Hamelin eating our food.

**Thorn :** We hate mice!

32

**Scratch :** Horrid little things.

**Fang :** We've driven them out of every storehouse and larder in Hamelin. They'll be hungry now. If you cats could turn a blind eye to anything we rats get up to, we'll bring every mouse in Hamelin to you.

*The rest of the rats and the cats seem surprised at this offer*

**Tom :** Every mouse?

**Sharkey :** Every mouse Chief? That seems a bit – mean.

**Captain :** It's dishonourable is what it is sir. Downright dishonourable.

**Fang :** So you don't want the mice then?

**Tom :** He didn't say that. *(pause, thinks)* You can really bring us every mouse?

**Fang :** I can.

**Sabretooth :** We can?

**Claw :** We can?

**Fang :** We can.

**Captain :** Dash it all it's a coward's trick.

**Sharkey :** I think so too. I don't like mice much, but it seems a bit cruel just to wipe them out.

**Sabretooth :** You really are the most pathetic excuse for a rat aren't you? Are you sure you're not just a fat mouse in disguise?

**Scratch :** That's a brilliant idea chief. We get rid of the mice and

33

keep the cats happen all at once.

**Bramble** : Survival of the fittest. It's just how nature works, and you can't fight nature.

**Kitty** : Mice. Oh can you imagine it?

**Tabby** : Tall ones.

**Fluff** : Small ones.

**Whiskers** : Mice with great big feet.

**Kitty** : Fluffy ones.

**Tabby** : Stuffy ones.

**Tom** : All that we can eat.

*The cats huddle together to discuss the idea. The rats also huddle together*

**Thorn** : You sure we can do this chief?

**Fang** : Sure I'm sure. All we have to do is set a trap.

**Sharkey** : A trap chief?

**Fang** : A bit of cheese. No mouse can resist cheese. It'll be easy as pie.

**Sabretooth** : Except it'll be the mice in the pie chief. *(rats laugh)*

**Kitty** : Can we trust the rats sir?

**Captain** : Never trust a rat sir. If there's one thing I've learned it's never trust a rat. No sense of honour sir.

*The cats and the rats leave their huddles*
34

**Tom :** All right. We accept. We'll turn a blind eye to anything you rats do. For now.

**Fang :** I thought you might. You just wait. You'll be dining on the finest mouse within the week.

**Tom :** We'd better be, otherwise we'll be dining on rat instead.

*the rats leave*

**Captain :** I think this is a very poor show sir.

**Tabby :** Oh do be quiet.

**Fluff :** Just think of all those mice.

**Whiskers :** I am thinking about them. I'm hungry already.

**Kitty :** I'm sure you won't say no to a nice big tasty mouse Captain.

**Captain :** Indeed I would say no ma'am. I like a mouse as much as the next cat, but I have principles. *(Captain stalks away)*

**Tom :** Let him go. He'll come back when we're feasting on roasted mouse.

**Fluff :** Mouse bake.

**Tabby :** Mouse cake.

**Kitty :** Grilled mouse.

**Whiskers :** Chilled mouse.

**Fluff :** Sage and onion filled mouse.

**Kitty :** Crispy mouse with lots of spice.

**Tabby :** Tender chocolate-coated mice.

**Whiskers :** Mice *au vin* and mice with jam,

**Kitty :** Mouse with nothing, mouse with stuffing.

**All cats :** Mouse with bacon, ham or veal,
Mouse for every single meal!

*The cats exit.*

## End of Act One.

## *ACT TWO*

**Scene one**

**Big Cheese's** *hideout. The mice are all curled up, asleep. Suddenly there is a clattering of pots and pans and* **Sharkey** *falls into the room.*

**Lulu :** *(shrieking)* A rat!

*All the mice wake up and scamper around, terrified.*

**Maisy :** Rats! Help!

**Twitch :** Run away! Run away!

**Sharkey :** Wait!

*The mice ignore* **Sharkey** *and head for the opposite exit. At that moment,* **Captain** *enters. The Mice all squeal again, trapped between* **Sharkey** *and* **Captain.**

**Truffle :** A cat!

**Squeaker :** The cats are coming!

**Snuffles :** I never thought the cats would get me!

**Big Cheese :** *(panicking more than anyone)* Cats! Rats! Oh me, oh my! Calamity! We'll all be eaten! Swallowed down like sweets!

**Sunny :** There's only one of them.

**Captain :** At ease! At ease! I'm not the enemy chaps.

**Sharkey :** *(surprised)* Me neither.

*The mice all pause and listen, all except* **Big Cheese** *who continues to run around panicking.*

**Big Cheese :** It's an attack! An invasion! We're all doomed! Doomed I tell you!

**Sharkey :** I just want to talk.

**Captain :** Same here, just a chinwag.

**Big Cheese :** I don't want to be eaten! Oh my tail and whiskers, what'll we do?

**Lulu :** Um, boss? I think we should listen.

**Big Cheese :** Listen to what? The terrible crunching sound as they grind my bones with their teeth?

**Sniffer :** The rat's alone.

**Squeaker :** So's the cat.

**Sunny :** I don't think they want to eat us boss.

37

**Big Cheese :** Alone?

**Lulu :** I think so boss.

**Big Cheese :** *(calming down)* Oh. Well. Obviously I can see they're alone. Yes. Just what I was going to point out.

**Twitch :** So what do they want?

**Big Cheese :** I was going to ask that. *(To Captain and Sharkey)* Now, just what's going on here? And don't try anything funny; I'm a master of unarmed combat.

**Squeaker :** That's right, he's completely armless.

*The mice close in around* **Captain** *and* **Sharkey.**

**Lulu :** So why are you here?

**Sharkey** *and* **Captain** *exchange glances.*

**Sharkey :** *(to Captain)* Good question. What are *you* doing here?

**Captain :** Me? I might ask you the same question old chap.

**Maisy :** Have either of you got anything to eat?

**Truffle :** I'm starving.

**Sharkey :** No, sorry.

**Big Cheese :** I told you, the Rats are storing a lot of supplies in one of the mayor's cellars. That's where we need to go. Squeaker saw them.

**Squeaker :** I did, but something smells fishy and I don't mean those barrels of sardines.

**Sharkey :** That's what I came to tell you. The other rats are setting a trap for you.

**Lulu :** A trap? Why?

**Sharkey :** They're going to give you to the cats.

**Squeaker :** The cats?

**Maisy :** To eat?

**Lulu :** No, as dancing partners. Well of *course* to eat.

**Captain :** That's what I was going to say too. I think it's a dashed underhanded thing to do.

**Big Cheese :** So we're supposed to believe you both want to help us?

**Snuffles :** The only thing cats ever want is to eat us.

**Twitch :** And everyone knows you can't trust a rat.

**Sharkey :** Look, I don't like what Fang's doing. We rats and mice have always got along okay haven't we? We're not much different really. Ears, whiskers, tails. I don't want to steal all the cheese.

**Captain :** A decent rat? I never heard of such a thing. I'm very glad to know you sir, very glad.

**Sharkey :** You seem honest enough too, for a cat.

**Captain :** I can't bear all this trickery. It's disgraceful. It my days cats and mice and rats knew where they were with each other. We weren't friends, but we respected one another.

**Snuffles :** Respect. These youngsters don't know the meaning of the word.

**Sharkey :** Why *can't* we be friends?

**Sunny :** That's what I was thinking.

**Captain :** What?

**Big Cheese :** Friends?

**Lulu :** With a rat?

**Twitch :** I'd sooner be friends with a beetle. In fact I am friends with a beetle. He's called Malcolm.

**Captain :** It just isn't done. Cats and rats and mice. Natural enemies.

**Sharkey :** Says who?

**Big Cheese :** Says everyone!

**Sharkey :** Well, I think everyone could be wrong. We don't have to fight. I don't like fighting.

**Snuffles :** I never thought I'd hear a rat say that.

**Captain :** By George, you know, the boy has a point. Although I do admit to finding mice jolly tasty.

**Lulu :** See! Cats want to eat us. They can't help themselves. They're just big, furry mouse eating machines. No offence.

**Captain :** None taken ma'am.

**Big Cheese :** We can't be friends with it, that's just the end of it. It wants to eat us, that's clear.

**Lulu :** While it thinks we're snacks we can't relax,
Or let it get too near.

**Squeaker :** It's eyeing my head to serve with some bread.
40

**Maisy :** It's going to pounce, I can see.

**Twitch :** It'll go for me next, then you I expect.

**Truffle :** And then it'll try eating me!

**Sharkey :** But he *isn't* trying to eat you.

**Captain :** I should say not. That just wouldn't be cricket.

**Big Cheese :** To be friends with the cats, or even the rats?
It just isn't done, I'd have said.

**Squeaker :** Spiders eat flies, and nobody tries,
To make them eat lettuce instead.

**Sharkey :** Well, I'd like to be your friend, and I don't care about
whether that's normal or not.

**Lulu :** It's the rules.

**Sharkey :** Who wrote the rules?

**Lulu :** I don't know. But rules are rules.

**Sharkey :** Well then they're silly rules.

**Sharkey** *exits crossly.*

**Captain :** Now that's a dashed decent fellow. *(pause)* Never thought
I'd say that
about a rat.

**Truffle :** *(Still unsure)* So you're really not going to eat us?

**Captain :** I'm not sure I could now I've met you all. You seem a
jolly nice bunch. I really don't think I can eat someone if I like them.

*The mice still seem uncertain.*

**Big Cheese :** Well then, I suppose thanks are in order.

**Lulu :** I'm not thanking a cat. Cats are trouble.

**Captain :** Anyway, must fly. Saucer of milk waiting and all that. Do watch out for those rats though. And the cats. Jolly nice to have met you all.

**Captain** *exits, leaving the mice confused.*

**Big Cheese :** Did I just dream that?

**Twitch :** I think they're lying boss. Probably in it together, trying to keep all the food for themselves.

**Lulu :** I think so too. You can't trust rats or cats. Everyone knows that.

**Sunny :** I don't know, they both seemed quite nice.

**Lulu :** Of course they did, that'll be part of the plan. Ha! We're too smart for their tricks.

**Truffle :** They're trying to scare us away from the cellar full of food, that's what they're doing.

**Twitch :** They must think we're really stupid.

**Squeaker :** What if they really do want to be friends?

**Sunny :** What if it really is a trap?

**Twitch :** Oh come on! A truthful rat and a cat that's not trying to eat us? That's about as likely as all the rats suddenly throwing themselves into the river, isn't it.

*The mice exit. Only* **Big Cheese, Sunny** *and* **Squeaker** *believe*

**Captain** *and* **Sharkey.**

**End of scene one.**

**Scene two.**

*The stage is in darkness. The sound of squeaking, scampering rats begins once again, followed by the shouts of the people.*

**Voice :** These rats! Why can't those useless cats catch them?

**Voice :** Come on Tom! Get the rats.

**Voice :** Maybe the cats are scared! Poor puss!

**Voice :** We have to do something, each morning there's more!

**Voice :** They're scampering over my dining room floor!

**Voice :** They've bitten my dog and my chicken won't lay.

**Voice :** There's a plague of them out there, all vicious and grey!

**Voice :** We must have assistance! We need a reprieve.

**Voice :** There must be an answer to make the rats leave.

**Voices together :** We need a solution! We need one today!
Won't somebody please make those rats go away!

*A shaft of light lands across the stage, and illuminated in the light it the unmistakable figure of the piper of Hamelin. He could be accompanied by a swift sound of music. Then silence and blackout.*

**End of scene two.**



**Scene three.**

*A storeroom. There is cheese and other food lying around.* **Thorn, Sabretooth, Scratch, Claw** *and the other rats lie in wait, hiding carefully behind the food.*

**Scratch :** *(Whispering)* Do you think they'll come?

**Sabretooth :** Of course they'll come. They're as dumb as the cats. Just smaller.

**Claw :** Just smaller.

**Thorn :** Shhhhh. Keep your voices down.

*The rats wriggle out of sight.* **Lulu, Snuffles, Maisy, Truffle, Twitch** *and any other mice enter quietly, looking around and sniffing.*

**Lulu :** Squeaker was right. Look at all this food!

**Twitch :** Cheese! Finally.

**Snuffles :** I never thought I'd never taste cheese again.

**Lulu :** Bread!

**Maisy :** Sausages!

**Truffle :** Cake!

44

**Lulu :** *(cautiously)* You don't suppose this could be, you know, a trap, do you?

**Twitch :** No chance! You know as well as I do you can't trust rats or cats. They're all as bad as each other.

**Lulu :** But what if they're not? What if some cats and rats are…*(pause, can't bring herself to say the word)* quite nice?

*The other mice start to laugh.*

**Twitch :** Quite nice! Cats and rats are just stupid, slobbering, mangy, ugly beasts and Hamlin would be better off without them

*As **Twitch** speaks, he finds himself facing one of the rats.*

**Truffle :** Rat!

**Snuffles :** They're everywhere!

**Maisy :** Run!

*The rats leap out and surround the mice. They have a net and the catch the mice inside it.*

**Sabretooth :** What was that about being stupid, slobbering, mangy, ugly beasts?

**Claw :** Ugly beasts.

**Twitch :** I didn't mean it. I like rats. I've always found you to be very kind. Very nice. Not the sort who would catch some harmless little mice in a net.

**Thorn :** Is this all the mice? There aren't very many.

**Sabretooth :** There'll be even less mice by the time the cats have eaten this lot.

45

**Claw :** This lot.

**Bramble :** This is nothing personal. It's just nature. Natural selection and all that, the strong prey on the weak.

**Scratch :** Yeah, and we don't like mice.

**Lulu :** Yeah, well, we don't like rats either! You're big and you smell.

**Sabretooth :** Well you're little and you squeak!

**Twitch :** You squeak too!

**Sabretooth :** We don't squeak. We growl. *(he gives a sort of growly squeak)*

**Snuffles :** You call that a growl? I've met scarier turnips!

**Sabretooth :** I'm real scary!

**Lulu :** You're not! You're big and lumbering and slow.

**Thorn :** We're not slow.

**Lulu :** Yes you are! There are snails that could outrun you. *Old* snails.

**Thorn :** No there aren't.

**Maisy :** Yes there are.

**Sabretooth :** We rats are famous for our speed. We could leave you little runts standing!

**Lulu :** No you couldn't. You couldn't even run a tap!

**Sabretooth :** Could!

46

**Twitch :** Prove it!

**Sabretooth :** All right, we will! *(pulls the net off the mice)* We'll soon see who's fastest. Faster than a cheetah I am. Faster than a speeding train. Legs of steel I've got!

**Bramble :** And the brains of a potato.

**Mice :** Bye!

*As* **Sabretooth** *brags, the mice escape.*

**Sabretooth :** Right. Now you'll see how fast I am.

**Thorn :** No, they'll see how stupid you are!

**Claw :** Stupid.

**Sabretooth :** *(not quite admitting he's been tricked)* They are pretty quick I guess.

**Scratch :** And you'd better do some pretty quick thinking before Fang asks you Why you let them go.

*The rats exit, chasing after the mice.*

**End of scene three.**

**Scene four.**

*The stage is in darkness.* **The Pied Piper's** *voice echoes out of the dark. It is gentle and melodious, with just a hint of cruelty. Pipe music begins very quietly as he speaks.*

**Pied Piper :**
Come rats of the town.
Come grey rats and brown.
Come to my call.
Come one and all.
Follow me follow,
Through forest and hollow.
In the street and the lane,
Hear my merry refrain.
See the river await,
And with it, your fate.
The water is flowing,
Onwards it's going.
Into the deep,
And eternal sleep.
Come swift and with speed.
Come follow my lead.
The music is calling,
And darkness is falling.

*The music continues to become louder.* **Scratch** *and* **Claw** *are drawn by it. They seem almost drunk.*

**Scratch :** I like that. It's a pretty tune.

**Claw :** Pretty tune. Very pretty tune.

**Scratch :** It's talking to me, the music. Is it talking to you?

**Claw :** Talking to me. Yes.

**Scratch :** I think it wants us to go this way. I'm coming. I can hear you.

*Both rats follow the music offstage, almost like zombies.*

**End of scene four.**

**Scene five.**

*A street in Hamlin.* **Lulu** *and* **Twitch** *run onto stage, looking over their shoulders. They are panting.*

**Lulu :** That rat was right. He's pretty fast.

**Twitch :** Do you think we've lost them?

**Lulu :** I hope so. *(looks around)* But I think we might have lost ourselves too.

**Sabretooth** *enters, not looking too pleased.*

**Sabretooth :** I've got you now, you little hairballs! I'm going to rip your tails off!

**Twitch :** *(backing away)* You win. You're quite right. You're very fast.

**Lulu :** Just like a cheetah. *Faster* than a cheetah.

**Twitch :** Way faster.

**Lulu :** Very impressive.

**Sabretooth :** *(flattered and confused)* Oh. Right.

**Lulu :** *(flattering him)* You didn't think we were really running away did you? We wouldn't dare run away from someone as fast and as clever as you!

**Sabretooth :** *(preening)* Of course not. No. I knew that.

**Twitch** *and* **Lulu** *exchange worried glances. At that moment, the*
49

*Piper's music begins to play. All three twitch their noses with interest.*

**Lulu :** That's a pretty tune.

**Twitch :** What is it?

**Lulu :** Do I look like a musician? I don't know. The nearest I get to a piano is when I'm gnawing its legs.

*The tune plays.* **Sabretooth** *begins to sway drunkenly, then staggers towards the exit.*

**Sabretooth :** I'm coming. I can hear you. I can hear you calling me. Can't you hear it calling?

**Lulu :** No.

**Twitch :** It's just music.

**Sabretooth :** I'm on my way. Keep singing. I'm coming to you.

**Sabretooth** *wobbles offstage.*

**Twitch :** Well that was odd. I thought we were both going to lose our tails.

**Lulu :** Something weird's going on. Let's go and find the others.

*Both exit.*

**End of scene five.**

**Scene six**

*The cats are all stretched out sleeping. There is the gentle sound of the pied piper's music in the air.*

**Kitty :** That's a very nice tune.

**Tabby :** It makes me want to dance.

**Whiskers :** It makes me want to sleep.

**Tom :** Any sign of those mice yet? I could just fancy a tasty little mouse.

**Fluff :** Haven't you noticed? The rats are all disappearing.

**Bramble** *enters, swaying and dancing to the music. Ignores the cats and staggers offstage, following the tune. The cats watch her go.* **Captain** *enters.*

**Captain :** There's some funny business going on in Hamlin and no mistake.

**Tom :** We noticed. All the rats are going nuts.

**Captain :** It's magic sir. That's what it is. That music sir, every time it plays, another rat vanishes. Just wander off and throw themselves in the river sir. Just like lemmings.

**Tabby :** Well, never mind. They're only rats. We won't miss them.

**Tom :** Good bye to the rats, they're all going bats.
And it looks like they're all going to drown.

**Kitty :** Oh what a shame, they're going insane.
There soon won't be any in town.

**Tabby :** Goodbye to the rats, They're not clever like cats.
It's nobody's fault but their own.

**Fluff :** If they hadn't gone wild and got people riled,
They'd all still be safely at home.

**Whiskers :** So ta-ta to the rats, they're finished at last,
Gone with a splash and a moan.

**Kitty :** We're not going to miss you.

**Tabby :** So don't pass a tissue.

**All cats :** Now Hamelin's a rodent-free zone!

**Captain :** I'm jolly ashamed that you'd rather play games,
When the rats are all lost in the water.
It's not right egad! We shouldn't be glad,
That those poor rats are heading for slaughter.

**Tom :** Oh for goodness sake, do we really care what happens to the rats?

**Captain :** That's not the point sir. It's the rats today, but it could be mice tomorrow,
or the children. Or us.

*The cats roll their eyes and settle down to sleep again.*

**Fluff :** Don't keep going on about it Captain.

**Whiskers :** I want to sleep. It's nice not having any rats to chase.

**Tom :** Pity about the mice though.

**Tabby :** I suppose we could always try to catch the mice for ourselves.

**Whiskers :** Or we could just go back to sleep.

**Thorn** *passes by, drawn by the music. She crosses the stage and disappears. The cats watch in disinterest.*

**Kitty :** There goes another one.

**Captain :** Dash it, I do feel like a cad. We should try to help.

**Tom :** Why? Best leave them to it. It's not our problem. We're not rats.

*The cats all go back to sleep.* **Captain** *exits, looking concerned.*


**End of scene six.**




**Scene seven.**

*The mice are celebrating.*

**Mice :**
The rats are all leaving, the roads are all heaving,
With masses of rats on the run!
Did you hear them all squeak,
As they race down the street?
Like bullets out of a gun!

The horrible rats are all making tracks,
They're off out of town by the score.
Did you hear them all pass,
Running over the grass?
And they're not coming back any more!


**Big Cheese :** Did you see them go?
53

**Squeaker :** It's amazing. I can hardly believe it. No more rats.

**Maisy & Truffle :** No more rats! No more rats!

**Snuffles :** I never thought I'd see the day Hamlin was free of rats.

**Sunny :** See, I said there was always a bright side.

**Big Cheese :** That piper fellow is doing us a huge favour.

**Lulu** *and* **Twitch** *join them.*

**Squeaker :** Hey you two, have you seen what's happening?

**Twitch :** Yeah, what's up with that? One of the rats just wandered off like he was sleepwalking.

**Maisy :** It's not just one rat.

**Truffle :** It's all the rats!

**Big Cheese :** Seems the people of Hamlin like the rats about as much as we do. They're being taken to the river.

**Twitch :** Why boss?

**Big Cheese :** Well why do you think dummy? For a picnic?

**Maisy :** I could just eat a picnic.

**Lulu :** Rats can't swim.

**Big Cheese :** Exactly.

**Squeaker :** They're sinking like stones.

**Truffle :** Grey, furry, overfed stones.

*The mice return to their celebrations.* **Twitch** *and* **Lulu** *look at each other with uncertainty.*

**Mice :**
Three cheers for the gent with the pipes that they sent,
To deal with the rat population.
He's charming them hither,
Off to the river.
And their watery extermination.

**Lulu :** *(quietly)* The rat wasn't lying.

**Big Cheese :** What?

**Twitch :** The rat. We thought the rat was lying about the trap. But he was telling the truth.

**Lulu :** He tried to help us.

*Slowly the other mice stop celebrating and think about this.*

**Maisy :** But rats can't be good.

**Twitch :** This one is.

*The sound of the piper's music fills the air. The mice all look a little ashamed of themselves.*

**Lulu :** Do you think, maybe, it's not a good thing, killing the rats?

**Truffle :** They're just rats.

**Lulu :** Maybe they're more like us than we want to admit.

**Truffle :** I'm nothing like a rat.

**Lulu :** *(pointedly)* No, you wouldn't bother to try and help a rat, would you? But that rat tried to help us.

**Maisy :** I wonder why.

**Sunny :** Maybe all rats and cats aren't the same. Maybe there are good ones and bad ones.

**Snuffles :** Suddenly I don't feel like celebrating any more.

**Squeaker :** Me neither.

**Big Cheese :** Are you all thinking what I'm thinking.

**Twitch :** That we should help them? Warn them?

**Big Cheese :** *(pause)* Actually, I was thinking we could get all the cheese back now, but I think your idea's better.

**Snuffles :** I never thought I'd see the day when I helped a rat.

*The Mice exit thoughtfully.*

**End of scene seven.**

**Scene eight.**

*The piper's music is heard and* **Fang** *and* **Sharkey** *enter, swaying hypnotically and following the sound. They reel around the stage a little. The sound of rushing water fades up.*

*The mice enter and spot the rats.*

**Big Cheese :** Hey! Hey rats! Stop!

**Twitch :** You're going to fall in the river!

**Lulu :** Stop!

*The rats ignore them.*

**Squeaker :** They're not listening!

**Maisy :** What can we do?

**Big Cheese :** Grab their tails! Quickly.

*The mice grab their tails and try to pull them back.*

**Lulu :** We're not strong enough.

**Sunny :** We have to try.

**Fang :** *(Dreamily)* What're you doing? Get out of our way.

**Twitch :** If you follow the music you'll fall in the river.

**Truffle :** And drown.

**Fang :** What music?

**Sharkey :** What river?

**Lulu :** It's like they're asleep.

**Squeaker :** The very loud pipe music that's getting louder all the time.

**Twitch :** And the very deep river over there.

**Fang :** Oh, *that* music. I like it. It's calling to me.

**Sharkey :** I can't see a river.

**Fang :** Is somebody pulling my tail?

**Sharkey :** It's not me chief.

**Big Cheese :** We can't stop them. They're too heavy.

**Snuffles :** It's all that stolen cheese! It's making them fat.

**Sunny :** We can't give up, c'mon boss, it's time for one of those brilliant ideas of yours.

**Big Cheese :** Brilliant ideas. *(thinks)* I'm all out of brilliant ideas right now.

**Lulu :** Oh what are we going to do?

*There is a loud meaow and a snarl and a hiss, and* **Captain** *enters. He leaps in front of* **Sharkey** *and* **Fang** *who seem to suddenly wake up, They both let out enormous squeals but* **Captain** *manages to pounce and catch* **Fang,** *pinning him to the ground.*

**Captain :** *(To the mice)* Well don't just stand there with your mouths open. Catch that rat!

*The mice realise that* **Sharkey** *is still heading for the river. They all leap at him, managing to hold him down.*

**Sharkey :** *(Struggling)* Get off. I want to follow the music.

**Snuffles :** I never thought I'd see the day when I sat on a rat.

**Big Cheese :** You'll thank us for this later.

**Lulu :** We hope.

**Fang :** Someone get this elephant off me!

**Captain :** Dash it all, stay still sir. I'm trying to do you a favour.

*The music reaches a crescendo and* **Sharkey** *and* **Fang** *continue to struggle.*

**Fang :** I hear the song of the wind in the trees.
Let me follow the music! I have to go, please!

**Sharkey :** I hear the song of the wind on the sea!
Exquisite and gentle it's calling to me.

**Fang :** The notes are like murmuring waves on a lake.

**Sharkey :** I feel like I'm dreaming although I'm awake.

**Fang :** Its drawing me onwards through colour and light.

**Sharkey :** Singing to me like the stars in the night.

**Fang :** I'm trying to come, but my legs feel like lead.

**Sharkey :** And somebody seems to be squashing my head.

*Finally the music dies away and* **Fang** *and* **Sharkey** *start to wake up.*

**Captain :** At last. I thought that infernal music would never stop.

**Big Cheese :** I think we did it. *(The mice cheer)*

**Snuffles :** I never thought I'd see the day I saved a rat.

**Fang :** *(Confused)* Can someone tell me why there seems to be a cat sitting on me?

**Lulu :** You were about to throw yourself into the river. We mice saved you. *(pause)* Well, Captain helped too.

**Fang :** The river? I wouldn't throw myself in the river!

59

**Captain :** Most of the other rats did I'm afraid sir. It was the music sir. 'Orrible business sir. Very underhanded.

**Sharkey :** You can get off me now. I'm not a cushion.

**Truffle :** If you were I'd get rid of you, you're very uncomfortable.

**Sharkey :** And you're squashing my tail.

**Sunny :** Look on the bright side, at least your tail isn't bobbing down the river with you still attached to it.

*The mice jump off him. They all look at each other suspiciously.*

**Big Cheese :** Well now, this is a first isn't it? Rats. Mice and a cat and none of us are trying to kill the others.

**Fang :** Not yet we're not.

**Captain :** You touch one of these brave mice sir, and I'll wear your tail for a belt, you see if I don't.

**Fang** *backs off.*

**Sharkey :** I think we had a lucky escape there Fang.

**Twitch :** We won't be making a habit of it mind.

**Fang :** I hate mice.

**Lulu :** I think the words you're looking for are "thank you."

**Fang :** I'm not thanking a mouse. Or a cat. I'm a rat. We're mortal enemies.

**Sharkey :** I don't see why we have to be.

**Fang :** That's because you're not a proper rat. It's the rules.

60

**Sunny :** What a pity there's no strong, brave, clever rat who could change the rules.

**Big Cheese :** Now don't be so silly. How could a *mere* rat change anything? It takes brains to change things.

**Lulu :** And courage.

**Captain :** And vision.

**Twitch :** And honour.

**Sharkey :** You're right. It's a shame there's no such rat leader. A leader like that would be respected. A leader like that would be admired all over Hamelin. Maybe all over the world. Don't worry about it Fang. It's just a shame you're too scared to change things.

**Big Cheese :** And too weak.

**Lulu :** And too stupid.

**Captain :** And too cowardly.

**Fang** *looks from* **Captain** *to the Mice, to* **Sharkey** *and back again.*

**Fang :** I didn't say I *couldn't* change the rules. Obviously I could, if I wanted to. Just a bit. Perhaps. There's nothing stopping me.

**Big Cheese :** Nothing at all.

**Captain,** *the mice and* **Sharkey** *cheer and* **Fang** *seems quite pleased.*

**Sharkey :** Nice one chief.

**Fang :** Maybe you mice aren't as dumb as I thought. Maybe we could get along.

**Big Cheese :** Maybe you rats aren't as mean as I thought,
Maybe I could have been wrong.

**Lulu :** Maybe you cats aren't as cruel as I thought.
Maybe it's time for a change.

**Captain :** Maybe you mice can do more than taste nice.
Would friendship be so very strange?

**Sharkey :** We could share all the cheese and the bread and the oats.

**Fang :** We could meet in the street and not grab at your throats.

**Twitch :** We could find a new way to live here together.

**Maisy :** We could all say "good morning" and "What lovely weather."

**Big Cheese :** Maybe it's time for some peace in this town?
To reach out our paws to each-other?

**Sharkey :** Maybe it's time for us all to be friends?
And maybe not eat one-another.

**Squeaker :** We could stop being scared at the sound of a purr.

**Captain :** We could stick to the snacks that have feathers not fur.

**Sunny :** We could look on the bright side when problems occur.

**Fang :** We could put all the food supplies back where they were.

**Big Cheese :** With that, my friend Fang, I would have to concur.

**Sunny :** Maybe its time for a good old group hug?

**Fang :** Don't push your luck.

**Snuffles :** I never thought I'd see the day when I was friends with a

62

rat.

**Captain :** Well there we are, new era of peace and harmony.

**Everyone :**
Maybe our differences aren't so extreme.
We're all more alike than we think.
We're not so dissimilar so it would seem,
And under our fur we all have the same dream.

**Captain :** To have some mouse steak with a drink?

**Everyone :** No!

**Captain :** Sorry. Just thinking out loud.

**End of scene eight**


**~ End ~**

Printed in Great Britain
by Amazon.co.uk, Ltd.,
Marston Gate.